Stand

Up

And

Tell

Them

by Crawford Howard, Billy Ritchie and Maud Steele

Edited by Liz Weir

Drawings by Doreen McBride

ADARE PRESS
White Gables
Ballymoney Hill
Banbridge
Telephone: Banbridge 23782

© 1991 Crawford Howard, Billy Ritchie and Maud Steele
Published by Adare Press
Typeset by Hallographics, Belfast
Printed by Romac Ltd., Belfast

ISBN 0 9516686 2 5

Stand Up and Tell Them

For generations past, the ability to stand up and tell a yarn has been a much admired talent at social gatherings throughout Ireland, and as as art form the traditional monologue or recitation has retained its popularity despite this 'high-tech' age. Many people will have memories of relatives delivering their favourite party pieces and even today one only has to quote a couple of lines from Service or Marshall and people will eagerly join in with their own fragments of memory. This collection aims to show that the tradition is very much alive, containing as it does samples of the work of three contemporary writers who are well known throughout Northern Ireland for their ability to capture both poignancy and humour in spoken verse. The pieces included are full of the rich Ulster dialect and as such are ideal for sharing — it is one thing to read them, but to obtain their full impact I suggest you read them ALOUD and preferably share them with friends! To prove that the poems do in fact reflect modern society with its stress and pressures one only has to consider the themes chosen — there are several examples which deal with the 'Troubles', continuing in the footsteps of the late James Young. Though our first contributor, Crawford Howard, often jokes about his ability to 'offend both sides in the one night', many of these pieces achieve much more than offence — often they force us to take a long hard look at ourselves and at how we view other people. Humour can often put across an important message, relieve tension, and put things into perspective, whether they involve domestic details or world politics! The best compliment that anyone can pay the writers of these verses is to stand up and tell the stories contained in the collection — we should be proud of our storytelling heritage and here in Ulster the performance of monologues has played a vital part in keeping the tradition alive. Hopefully these pieces will be performed for many years to come!

Liz Weir
Ahoghill
September 1991

Contents

Crawford Howard

'The Steam Trap is doin' its job'.

Crawford Howard is well known in Northern Ireland as a storyteller and a musician. Many of his stories are told in song form as well as verse. His yarns are full of real life experiences but Crawford's quirky sense of humour has led him to make certain changes to the norm and to show just what effect an injection of imagination can do.

The Diagonal Steamtrap

Now they built a big ship down in Harland's —
She was made for to sell to the Turks —
And they called on the Yard's chief designer
To design all the engines and works.

Now finally the engines was ready
And they screwed in the very last part
An' yer man says, 'Let's see how she runs, lads!'
An' bejasus! the thing wouldn't start!

So they pushed and they worked an' they footered
An' the engineers' faces got red
And the designer he stood lookin' stupid
An' scratchin' the back of his head.

But while they were fiddlin' and workin'
Up danders oul' Jimmie Dalzell.
He had worked twenty years in the 'Island'
And ten in the 'aircraft' as well.

So he pushed and he worked and he muttered,
Till he got himself through till the front
And he has a good look roun' the engine
An' he gives a few mutters and grunts,

And then he looks up at the Gaffer
An' says he, 'Mr. Smith, d'ye know?
They've left out the Diagonal Steam Trap!
How the hell d'ye think it could go?'

Now the engineer eyed the designer
And the designer he looks at the 'hat'
And they whispered the one to the other,
'Diagonal Steam Trap? What's that?'

But the Gaffer, he wouldn't admit like
To not knowin' what this was about,
So he says, 'Right enough, we were stupid!
The Diagonal Steam Trap's left out!'

Now in the meantime oul' Jimmie had scarpered
— away down to throw in his boord —
And the Gaffer comes up and says, 'Jimmy!
D'ye think we could have a wee word?'

'Ye see that Diagonal Steam Trap?
I know it's left out — it's bad luck,
But the engine shop's terrible busy
D'ye think ye could knock us one up?'

Now, oul' Jimmy was laughin' his scone off.
He had made it all up for a geg
He seen what was stoppin' the engine —
The feed-pipe was blocked with a reg!

But he sticks the oul' hands in the pockets
An' he says, 'Aye, I'll give yez a han'.
I'll knock yez one up in the mornin'
An' the whole bloody thing will be grand!'

So oul' Jim starts to work the next morning
To make what he called a Steam Trap,
An oul' box an' a few bits of tubing
An a steam gauge stuck up on the top,

An' he welds it all on till the engine
And he says till the wonderin' mob,
'As long as that gauge is at zero
The Steam Trap is doin' its job!'

Then he pulls the reg outa the feed pipe
An, he gives the oul' engine a try
An' 'bejasus! she goes like the clappers
An' oul Jimmy remarks, 'that's her nye!'

Now the ship was the fastest seen ever,
So they sent her away till the Turks
But they toul' them, 'That Steam Trap's a secret!
We're the only ones knows how that works!

'But the Turks they could not keep their mouths shut
An' soon the whole story got roun'
An' the Russians got quite interested —
Them boys has their ears till the groun'!

So they sent a spy dressed as a sailor
To take photies of Jimmy's Steam Trap
And they got them all back till the Kremlin
An' they stood round to look at the snaps.

Then the head spy says, 'Mr Kosygin!
I'm damned if I see how that works!'
So they sent him straight off to Siberia
An' they bought the whole ship from the Turks!

When they found the Steam Trap was a 'cod', like',
They couldn't admit they'd been had,
So they built a big factory in Moscow
To start makin' Steam Traps like mad!

Now Kosygin rings up Mr. Nixon
And he says, 'Youse'uns thinks yez are great!
But wi' our big new Russian-made Steam trap
Yez'll find that we've got yez all bate!

'Now oul Nixon, he nearly went 'harpic',
So he thought he'd give Harland's a call
And he dialled the engine-shop number
And of course he got sweet bugger all!

But at last the call came through to Jimmy
In the midst of a terrible hush,
'There's a call for you here from the 'White House!'
Says oul' Jim, 'That's a shop in Portrush!'

There's a factory outside of Seattle
Where they're turnin' out Steam Traps like Hell
It employs twenty-five thousand workers
And the head of it — Jimmy Dalzell!

Crawford Howard

8

The Arab Orange Lodge

(This poem may be sung to the air: 'The Wearing of the Green')

A loyal band of Orangemen from Ulster's lovely land,
They could not march upon the 12th — processions was all banned,
So they flew off till the Middle East this dreadful law to dodge
And they founded in Jerusalem the Arab Orange Lodge

Big Ali Bey who charmed the snakes he was the first recruit,
John James McKeag from Portglenone learned him till play the flute
And as the oul' Pied Piper was once followed by the rats
There followed Ali till the lodge ten snakes in bowler hats.

They made a martial picture as they marched along the shore.
It stirred the blood when Ali played 'The fez my father wore'
And Yussef Ben Mohammed hit the 'lambeg' such a bash
It scared the living daylights from a camel in a sash!

Now the movement spread both far and wide — there were lodges by
    the score.
The 'Jerusalem Purple Heroes' was the first of many more,
The 'Loyal Sons of Djeddah' and the Mecca Purple Star'
And the 'Rising Sons of Jericho' who came by motor car.

The banners too were wonderful and some would make you smile
— King Billy on his camel as he splashed across the Nile —
But the Tyre and Sidon Temperance had the best one of them all
For they had a lovely picture of Damascus Orange Hall!

The Apprentice boys of Amman marched beneath the blazing sun,
The Royal Black Preceptory were negroes every one
And Lodges came from Egypt, from the Abu Simbel Falls,
And they shouted 'No surrender!' and 'We'll guard old Cairo's walls!'

But when the ban was lifted and the lodges marched at last
The Arabs all decided for till march right through Belfast
And they caused a lot of trouble before they got afloat,
For they could not get the camels on the bloody Heysham boat!

9

Now camels choked up Liverpool and camels blocked Stranaer
And the Sheik of Kuwait came along in his great big motor car,
But the 'Eastern Magic' L.O.L. they worked a crafty move.
They got on their magic carpets and flew into Aldergrove!

When they came to Castle Junction where once stood the wee Kiosk,
They dug up Royal Avenue to build a flamin' mosque
And Devlin says to Gerry Fitt, 'I think we'd better go!'
There's half a million camels coming down from Sandy Row.

The speeches at the 'field' that day were really something new,
For some were made in Arabic and some were in Hebrew,
But just as Colonel Nasser had got up to sing 'The Queen',
I woke up in my bed at home and found it was a dream!

Crawford Howard

The Flying Fitter

A big lad came to work in the 'Aircraft',
So the lads took him out for some beers,
And soon they were calling him 'Dumbo',
Because of the size of his ears.

But after a couple of hours, like,
They had to face up till the truth.
There wasn't no two ways about it,
Big Dumbo was only a 'drouth'.

He was knockin' back 'half uns' like water,
And wee Jimmy looks up and says 'Hi!
If you take any more ye'll be flyin' !
'He sez, 'Listen, oul' han', I CAN fly!

'Sez wee Jim 'D'ye mean yez a pilot?'
Well, I just hope that I'll be around,
The next time you're goin' up solo,
When ye get thon big lathe off the ground!'

The big lad says, 'I need no airplane!
Ye see when I go on the tear
An' I get a few bottles an' half 'uns,
I can just go straight up in the air!'

Well the whole place went into hysterics
To think of the very idea
An' the big lad got red in the face, like,
An' he says to wee Jim 'Houl' my beer!'

Then he takes a buck lep on the counter.
The lads could do nothin' but laugh,
But he gives a few flaps with his ears, like,
And bejasus! the bugger takes aff!

An' before ye could knock back a half 'un,
He was buzzin' about roun' the light,
Like a flamin' great moth roun' a lantern
Ye would see on a good summer night

An' then he swoops down on wee Jimmy
An' he snatches the beer from his hand,
An he hovers about roun' the counter
Sez wee Jim, 'He's goin' in for to land!'

But landing was not in his programme
The window was open, you see,
So he flutters straight out through the window
An' shouts 'I'm for Donaghadee!'

Now the lads was all struck wi' amazement.
They said, 'where has he got till at all?'
Then wee Jim yells, 'Bejasus, I see him!
He has lit on the oul' City Hall!'

And right enough there he was perchin'
About eighty five feet off the ground,
Sharing his 'piece' with the pigeons
And the starlings all flutterin' round.

Says wee Jim, 'We'll sneak up on him aisy!
If you come up too quick he'll take fright.
Put a bottle of beer on the windy
An' mebbe he'll roost there all night!'

But before any of the lads could get near him
He shot away up in the air.
Sez wee Jim, 'I would not have believed it
If I had not of had of been there!'

But yer man he went higher an' higher
Till he disappeared over the town.
Sez wee Jim, 'I still think he's for landin'
For the flaps of his trousers is down!'

'Now you've heard of them astronaut Yankees,
They left a wireless set on the moon.
It sends back all oul' daft information
Like if it's going to blow up, an' how soon.

They were sitting one night at Cape Kennedy,
When a fella wi' phones on his head
sez, 'There's a voice comin' down from the moon here
But I couldn't make out what it said.'

Then up steps a fella from Belfast
Sez he, 'Sure there's nothin' to that.
It said, 'Two by the neck and a half 'un!
And make sure that the half 'un is hot!'

Then the voice in the headphones continued
And said, 'God, but my head's awful thick!
Tell Shorts I'll be in on the Monday,
But till then I will be on the sick!'

Now, it seems that yer man got off coorse like
— that full that he could'nt half see—
An' he found he had lit on the moon, like,
Instead of in Donaghadee!

Now I know of some of you won't believe this.
Ye'll think the whole story's a 'cod'.
It's as true as that Paisley's a 'Mickey'
Or as true as the Pope is a 'Prod'.

Crawford Howard

The Rebel Record-player

Wee Willie John McFadyean was a loyal Orange 'Prod',
And he thought that Ian Paisley was just one step down from God.
He thought they ate the 'childer' in the backwoods of Ardoyne,
And he knew that history started with the Battle of the Boyne!

One night he took a brick in his hand and he wandered up the 'Falls'.
He was muttering 'Up the Rangers!' and humming 'Derry's Walls!'
He bust a big shop window, to annoy the Pope of Rome
And he took a record player out and then he staggered home.

Next night they held a 'hooley' in the local Orange Hall
And Willie took his player to make music at the ball.
He chose a stack of records of a very loyal kind,
But when the music started up he nearly lost his mind!

For the Fenian record-player was a rebel to the core,
It played the tunes that Orange Hall had never heard before.
For 'Derry's Walls' and 'Dolly's Brae' it didn't care a fig,
And it speeded up 'God Save The Queen' till it sounded like a jig!

It played the 'Boys of Wexford' and 'The Wearing of the Green'.
Such turmoil in an Orange Hall has never yet been seen.
It played the 'Woods of Upton' and 'The Men of '98',
But when it played 'The Soldier's Song' it sealed wee Willie's fate.

For the boys went clean demented — to the ground wee Will was thrown,
And they kicked his ribs in one by one to the tune of 'Garryowen'.
They threw him out the window to a 'Song of Old Sinn Fein',
And they kicked him all down Sandy Row to 'A Nation Once Again!'

Wee Willie's up in Purdysburn — he's crazy as a coot,
He just sits there in his padded cell and tootles on his flute,
And when he tries to play 'The Sash' he always gets it wrong,
For halfway through he always finds he's playing 'The Soldier's Song'.

There's a moral to this story — what it is I cannot say,
It may be just the ancient one that crime will never pay.
If you ask wee Will McFadyean he says, 'Ah, crime be blowed!'
'If you want to pinch a record-player do it up the Shankill Road!'

Crawford Howard

The Foodaholic

There once was an oul' alcoholic
That lived up the Cliftonville Road.
His behaviour was quite diabolic
An' he niver left 'til he was 'throwed'
Outa every pub in the district
'till the doctor said, 'If ye don't stop
Inside of six months at the latest
You will definitely be for the chop!'

Now this scared the oul' eejit stupid
So' he never went into a pub
But the funny thing was, like, whatever the cause, like,
He began getting drunk on his grub!
Now this was a strange situation
For if he got a mouthful o' tae
Or a good bowl of soup his head started to droop
An' the wife would say, 'God, he's away!'

Sez the wife one night, 'See thon oul' grocer?
I'd like to get him by the hair
For he stood thon oul' eejit an onion
An' now he's away on the tear!'
An' you know where they found the oul' geezer?
That full that he couldn't half stan'
Lyin' across a deep freezer
Wi' a fish finger clutched in his han'.

But then he fell into bad company
For he met an oul' fool like himself,
That got rotten on jelly an' custard
Or whatever he pinched off the shelf
And they'd get themselves begfuls o' toffee
An' sit gettin' plastered all day,
Standin' each other black coffee
An' fightin' about which one would pay.

They were soon known all round the district
An' they thought it was terrible hard
If they went in to get a fish supper
They were always told, 'Sorry, you're barred!'
And the poor Chinese waiters would worry
For they all knew just what to expect,
If yer men hit the chow mein and curry
They knew that the whole place would get wrecked!

But one night yer men overdone it.
They had two pasties over the eight
An' they borrowed a car 'till get home, like'
For they knew it was terrible late,
An' of course they were stopped by a peeler
Who started to shout and to 'barge'
An' he says, 'Yez have both done it this time!
Yer arrested for bein' drunk in charge!'

Now the oul' fellas stood up in Court like,
An' they said, 'We have got this rap bate!
Yez have made out the charge sheet all wrong, like,
We were not drunk — we were ate!'
An' ye'll still see them most Sunday mornings
As they wait to get in for a 'cure',
Standin' about with their tongues hangin' out
An' bangin' the grocer's back door!

Crawford Howard

The Young Rebel

(This poem may be sung to the air: 'Down by The Green Bushes')

As I was a-walking through Belfast one day
I met a young rebel who to me did say,
'I bet you a "fiver" one thing you won't try!
Wear your sash up the "Falls" on the 12th of July'.

Says I, 'My young shaver I bet you I will'.
Says he, 'If you do then it's you they will kill
For there's one thing to do if you're ready to die —
Wear your sash up the "Falls" on the 12th of July'.

So I walked up the 'Falls' from beginning to end.
With my sash on my back I was greeted as a friend
I collected my 'fiver' and still didn't stop
With my sash on my back and my coat on the top!

'Now', says I my young rebel 'now here's my reply'.
'You can have your cash back if three things you will try'
'Shout "Up the Republic!" and "The Border must go!" '
'And "To hell with King Billy!" going down Sandy Row!'

'Ah', says he, 'sure that's easy! I'll do it today!'
And I prayed for his soul as he wandered away.
He was back in an hour (without the police)
And to my surprise he was still in one piece!

So I gave him his money and shook him by the hand
And said. 'How did you do it, for I don't understand?'
'If you'd shouted those things they'd have kicked you to death!'
'Ah', says he, 'Sure I shouted them under my breath!'

Now the moral of this story is plain to be seen.
There are many smart fellows, both Orange and Green.
Be it St. Patrick's day or the 12th of July
If you play with the head, sure you'll always get by!

Crawford Howard

17

Song of Belfast

(This poem may be sung to the air: 'Song of the Clyde')

I'll sing you a song of the town of Belfast,
Where the oul' Union Jack is still nailed to the mast,
But the flag-pole is shaking with every blast
Oh! a wonderful town is the town of Belfast.
We've wonderful factories and shipyards as well
So to keep up employment we'll blow them to Hell
For in bullets and bombs the resources are vast
And the bullet and bomb sing the song of Belfast

Chorus:
Poor oul' Belfast — how long can it last
For there's bits disappearing with every blast
It may have no future but boy! what a past,
A wonderful town is the song of Belfast.

Now in Belfast there's more than the weasel goes 'pop'
For there's smashing reductions in every shop.
I know a wee lad took his girl to a ball
They went in through the door and came out through the wall!
It's not even safe to go into a pub
For the bits of glass flying would slice off yer gub.
I went out last night for a couple of beers
And bejasus! the lounge bar came down round my ears!

And there was little Willie who to please King Billy hit a poor oul'
Mickey on the head.
There was little Seamus — he will soon be famous — he blew up a
van of Ormo bread,
·There was Sean and Michael on a motor cycle flying up and down the
Springfield Road
And they're throwing boulders at the British soldiers who are only
doing what they are told.

18

There was Bernadette — I'm sure she's talkin' yet — I seen her on the
  Telly-V
And by all the powers they went on for hours and hours by courtesy
  of B.B.C.
There was all the talkers minus Brian Falkner like big Ian P. and Gerry
  Fitt
But I know a fellow who was watching 'tele' said they talked an awful
  lot of rubbish.

Chorus

Now the poor starving masses all stand in a daze
When they hear of the things that go on in the Maze,
For the fellas in there don't like eating at all,
For they keep throwin' their dinners out over the wall.
Now the doctor's say walking is good for your health
But bejasus! it's not like you walk on the '12th'
And if you get lifted — what a terrible fate!
You get sent up the Crumlin until ye escape!

Crawford Howard

19

The Breadman

(This poem may be sung to the air: 'Jesse James')

Willie Thompson was a man who drove an Ormo van.
He sold the best of bread.
He didn't make much money but this wasn't very funny
For the wife could never get him out of bed.

Chorus
Now poor Willie's dead and gone
But his fame still lingers on.
He drove the fastest breadvan in Belfast
And he had three mighty sons all brought up on Paris buns
And they'll all be driving breadvans till the last.

Through flame and shot and shell Willie drove his breadvan well.
He didn't give a damn for the I.R.A.
Till one morning up the 'Falls' he was whistling 'Derry's Walls'
And they swore they'd drive his poor old van away.
Willie jumped down from the van and a battle soon began.
Vienna rolls and 'crusties' he did fling
And amidst the flying bread, where men lay cold and dead
They stood amazed to hear old Willie sing:

'With a gun, with a gun
Ah ye can't get a van with a gun!
You can take yer oul' revolver And shove it over the Border
But you can't get a van with a gun!'

Now many a man lay dead with a pan loaf through his head
Or murdered by a flying Paris bun.
There was very few would dare to face a flying current square
And the I.R.A. were falling one by one,
Then a sharp Vienna roll it took its deadly toll
And Willie lay spreadeagled on the ground
And the poor old van was made into a barricade
And the spent pan loaves was lyin' all around.

Chorus

When the nights are cold and dark, where the Ormo bread-vans park
They say that Willie's presence you can feel.
You can hear his eerie calls as he sets off for the Falls,
In a ghostly van with Willie at the wheel,
And the British Army say, as they fight the I.R.A.
Old Willie's ghost is worth a thousand men,
For the Provos all keep clear and the Officials shake with fear
When they hear that Willie Thompson rides again
And on that final morn when old Gabriel blows his horn
To rouse the mighty company of the dead.
If you see an Ormo van and St. Peter's buying a 'pan'
It's only Willie Thompson selling bread!

Crawford Howard

Dixon From Dungannon

Now Dixon from Dungannon was a man of great renown.
Whenever things were going wrong around Dungannon town
If yer oul' lawnmower was busted, or yer biro wouldn't write,
Then Dixon from Dungannon was the man to put it right.

The big air-show at Farnborough — a new jet was on show.
Prince Phillip and the Queen was there, but the jet just would not go,
An' this big lad dandered out and he fixed her at a stroke
An' then he shouts up till the Queen, 'They forgot about the choke!'

Prince Philip turns round all amazed to where the Queen was stan'in,
But she says, 'Don't be daft oul' han'! That's Dixon from Dungannon!'
An' then she shouts, 'Hi! Dixon! Go home and get your Alice!
And bring her roun' about half-nine for a party at the palace!'
The palace was in darkness when he brought oul' Alice roun'
And the Queen says, 'Could ye fix that fuse, like, before we all sit
   down?'
So he fixed the fuse and they all sat down and began to smack their
   lips
As they ate the Royal pastie and chewed the Royal chips.

A volcano up in Iceland was causin' lots of trouble,
So of course they sent for Dixon an' he got there at the double.
He says, 'Where's this volcano, for I'm the man til bate 'er
An' he got a lump of bubble gum an' stuffed it down the crater.
He then stood back and wiped his hands and says, 'Now calm yer
   fears!
I reckon that'll houl' her for about a thousand years!'
An' right enough it held her — now for miles around they come,
To watch her blowing bubbles outa Dixon's bubble-gum!

The Yankees was all very proud of their rocket till the moon.
When they found they couldn't get her back — that made them
    change their tune!
So mission-control Houston, they sent word to Mr. Nixon
An' he says, 'There's just one thing to do! We'll send a wire to Dixon!
The reply came back from Dixon — 'Thon oul' rockets just a wreck!
But adjust yer carburettor, lads, an' that'll get her back!'
So they fixed the carburetter and they muttered 'That's her now!'
— But Dixon from Dungannon was the man that showed them how!

Now poor oul Dixon died last week and up to Heaven he went.
St. Peter says, 'You can't come in, like — Ye wouldn't be content
There's never nothing wrong in here — there's nothin' needin' fixin'.
With that the Devil wanders up — Says he, 'Is your name Dixon?
For if it is come on with me — you know we'll treat you well.
There's a few wee jobs needs doing on the left hand gate of Hell!'
So Dixon says, 'Right! I'm yer man!' and with the Devil aff he goes
And what the Devil happened then the Devil only knows
But if things is goin' wrong in Hell, ye can bet until this day,
That Dixon from Dungannon won't be very far away!

Crawford Howard

The Suction Man

(This poem may be sung to the air: 'The Hills of Connemara')

There was a sweep in Belfast town,
Who swept the chimney all around,
His old brush walloped up and down
In the good oul' town of Belfast.

He heard about a 'suction man'
Who had a most terrific plan.
He sucked the soot intil a big tin can
In the good oul' town of Belfast.

Chorus
So gather up your brushes in your old black van,
Sweep the chimney while you can,
Run like the devil from the 'suction man'
In the good oul' town of Belfast.

So yer man got the engine off an old Ford van
And he coupled it up to a bloody great can
And he pressed the button and begod! it ran!
In the good old town of Belfast.

He says, 'Hi missus! Can I sweep yer flue?
You'll see what this machine can do.
Yes chimney will be just like new
In the good old town of Belfast!'

Chorus

So he pressed the button and he let her go.
It was a most terrific show,
Where the stuff all came from I don't know,
In the good old town of Belfast.

There was dried cement and bits of brick,
The clouds of soot would make you sick,
Oul' birds nests and begs of sticks
In the good old town of Belfast.

Chorus

Now round the room the oul' doll hopped.
When she seen the mess she nearly dropped
But the oul' lad could not get it stopped
In the good old town of Belfast.

It sucked a hole right through the wall,
It sucked down chimney pots and all,
And the whole damn place began to fall
In the good old town of Belfast.

Chorus

From a 'Co-op' shop across the street
It sucked out pounds and pounds of meat.
It sucked the oul' lad off his seat
In the good oul town of Belfast.

The sweep began to shout and curse.
Says he, 'I'll try it in reverse!
It may be better and it can't be worse
In the good old town of Belfast!'

Chorus

So he hit the oul' gear-stick a swipe
And the stuff went flying back up the pipe.
There was clouds of soot and pounds of tripe
In the good old town of Belfast.

The forecast was for snow and sleet
And clouds at seven thousand feet,
But it never mentioned the lumps of meat
In the good old town of Belfast.

Chorus

A jet plane then a report did make
And it said, 'Send help for Jasus sake!
I've just been hit by a pound of steak
About the town of Belfast!'

A helicopter flying low
Was hit by liver from the 'Co'
And a flying sausage killed a crow
Above the town of Belfast.

Chorus

But worse things were to happen yet.
The sweep admitted he was 'bet'
When a chop brought down a jumbo-jet
In the middle of the town of Belfast.

Now the sweep was sentenced by the courts.
By a great big firm his machine was bought,
And they use it as a wind-tunnel down in Shorts,
In the good old town of Belfast.

Chorus

Now the oul' doll she recovered well.
But the suction-man still casts a spell
For when she sees one she runs like hell
All round the town of Belfast.

Chorus

Crawford Howard

The Sloping Beauty

(This poem may be sung to the air: 'Let Him Go Let Him Tarry)

'Once there was an oul' doll who was bendy at the knees.
She sloped down from the shoulders at forty-five degrees,
Her shape was somethin' shockin' — it really would annoy,
She was called the 'Slopin Beauty' from Belfast to Aughnacloy.

Chorus
She is the 'Slopin' Beauty' from the town of old Belfast.
The medical profession all look at her aghast.
The Leaning Tower of Pisa has not been worth a damn
Since it seen the 'Slopin' Beauty' slopin' aff a Shankill tram.

And when she went out for a walk it always was her fate,
That people went to houl' her up when she was walkin' straight,
And when she went to bed at night her parents always found
They thought she was sittin' up when she was lyin' down

Chorus

She disappeared from work one day when feeling discontent.
Her oul' lad called the polis 'till find out where she had went.
But when he told the sergeant all he done was laugh,
Sez he 'The Slopin' Beauty would appear to have sloped aff!'

Chorus

She went intil a restaurant when comin' home from work.
The oul' lad sittin' next to her he nearly went beserk.
He shouted for the manager — he was in an awful state.
'Get that oul' doll outa here — her face is in me plate!'

Chorus

The Slopin Beauty's dead and gone — her soul they tried to save,
And then they tried to bury her — she would not fit the grave.
So then they dug her up again and stuck her in a cavity.
She's the only corpse in Belfast that defies the law of gravity!

Chorus

Crawford Howard

Happy Christmas Belfast

Father Christmas was sittin' in Iceland,
He lives there, like, everyone knows.
He was toastin' his toes by the fire
And muttering, 'Good luck 'till yez, toes!'
Mrs. Christmas come in wi' a letter.
Says she, 'The post's landed at last!'
Father Christmas took one look and shuddered,
And says 'My God! The post-mark's Belfast!'

Mrs. Christmas 'rared up' like a tiger.
'You're not going back there no more!
Ye remember what happened ye last time.
Ye arrived back in Iceland half tore!
An' the turkey was burnt to a cinder,
An' you lyin' full in the sleigh,
An' you fell in the arm-chair half stupid,
An' I put the reindeer away.'

Father Christmas looked suitably sheepish,
'I got lost goin' over the hills.
I went down thon big chimney with smoke comin' out,
Sure I didn't know it was Bushmills!
And the heat and the fumes of the whiskey,
An' me only out of my bed,
An' what with one thing an' another,
The whole thing went straight to my head.'

Mrs. Christmas says, 'Bushmills yer granny!
Ye never were there in yer puff!
Ye were rakin' around with them winos in town
Sure ye never could get half enough!
Ye were seen staggerin' 'full' outa Kelly's
Wi' thon three oul' men from the East,
An' you drove the oul' sleigh down Chapel Lane the wrong way,
An' nearly ran over a priest.'

Father Christmas says 'Give us the letter!
I've had just enough of your chat!
You've a tongue on ye worse nor your mother
An' there's not nothin' worser nor that!'
(Father Christmas's grammar was suspect
Though he went to a very good school —
The famous North Pole Comprehensive —
They don't turn out mugs as a rule.)

Father Christmas tore open the letter,
Then he started to laugh like a drain,
An' he says to the wife, 'This'll kill ye!
It's thon wee lad from Belfast again!
Do you know what he's askin' for this time?
It isn't a train or a bike.
He wants me to make them stop fightin'
In Belfast for Christmas, like!'

Mrs. Christmas says 'Make them stop fightin'?
There's no mortal body could do it
But still, though, you'll have to do somethin'
Or else they'll all say you have blew it!
You remember thon bottle of powder
Thon traveller left here thon day?
An' you thought it was only a gimmick
An' it's kickin' about in the sleigh?'

'And the label says, 'Full Strength Peace Powder',
And you sprinkle it over their heads,
An' it makes them feel all 'palsy-walsy' —
At least that's what the traveller said!'
Father Christmas says, 'Heavens, we'll try it!
I'd better get weavin' the day.
Get out there an' harness them reindeer,
An' throw my red suit in the sleigh!'

29

He was over Belfast in ten minutes.
He travelled so fast it would blind ye!
But as he said, 'Them reindeer can motor
If ye get a good tail wind behind ye!'
But in slowin' down over the city
He just missed a terrible fate.
He was nearly run down by the shuttle
That was comin' in two hours late!

But at last he got into position
And he opened a kind of trap-door,
An' he emptied the bottle of powder
Right down through the hole in the floor,
And as it fell down on the city
The effect was immediate and drastic!
Father Christmas looked down in amazement,
And he says, 'This is fan-flippin'-tastic!'

Ian Paisley was sending out Christmas cards,
With tidings of gladness and hope,
And he sent one to Margaret Thatcher
And begod! He sent two to the Pope!
Yes, he sent one to Margaret Thatcher
Saying, 'Dear Maggie, Ulster says "Yes"
And as for your Anglo-Irish agreement;
I hope it's a roaring success!'

Some powder blew right down to Dublin
And it filtered through into the Dail.
Charlie Haughey grabbed Garrett Fitzgerald
And they both did a dance in the aisle.
Then they thought that a drink was in order
So they headed for Guinness's brewery
But Garrett says, 'Charles, get your motor!
The booze is far cheaper in Newry!'

Cardinal O'Fiaich got a sniff of the powder
And he did what you might think was rash.
He decreed that each Catholic church sevice
Should begin (and conclude) with the 'Sash'.
The Hibernians marched up the Shankill,
The Orangemen marched up the Falls,
Sammy Wilson saluted the tricolour,
And John Hume was bawlin' 'Derry's Walls'.

But up in the sky over Belfast
Father Christmas was chuckling with glee,
As the oul' rein-deer started to gallop
An' he headed back home for his tea,
An' he smiled as the city grew smaller
And muttered, 'How long will it last?
But a few days of peace — you deserve it —
So here's "Happy Christmas, Belfast"'.

Crawford Howard

Violetta

(This poem may be sung to the air: 'Johnny Lad')

Once there was an oul' doll who worked down in the 'Co',
Her name was — Violetta — and she came from Sandy Row.
Singing, 'Oh would ye go and are ye comin' out?
I'll buy ye fifty tatie farls and half a pint of stout!'

Her husband was an oul' lad who worked down in the yard.
There was not a pub in Belfast from which he was not barred.
Singing, 'Oh would ye go and are ye comin' out?
I'll buy ye fifty tatie farls and half a pint of stout!'

And every Friday evening wherever he chanced to roam,
You'd hear him singing this oul' song as he came rolling home,
'Hear my song, Violetta, hear my song beneath the moon
Put the pan on, Violetta, for I will be home soon!'

Now Violetta's temper was gettin' more ferocious,
For she was always sober and he was always stocious,
Singing, 'Oh would ye go and are ye comin' out?
I'll buy ye fifty tatie farls and half a pint of stout!'

So one night in a temper she kicked him out of bed.
She grabbed the bloody frying pan and bate him round the head.
Singing, 'Oh would ye go and are ye comin' out
I'll buy ye fifty tatie farls and half a pint of stout!'

Then she grabbed the bottle of whiskey and put it 'till her head
And danced around the kitchen singing fit to wake the dead,
Singing, 'Oh would ye go an' are ye comin' out
I'll buy ye fifty tatie farls and half a pint of stout!'

Then she found she liked the taste of it as she poured it down her
   throttle,
So she ran down 'till the corner pub and brought another bottle,
Singing, 'Oh would ye go and are ye comin' out?
I'll buy ye fifty tatie farls and half a pint of stout!'

Now the moral of this story, it really can't be missed
For the oul' lad's always sober now and she is always drunk
Singing, 'Oh would ye go and are ye comin' out?
I'll buy ye fifty tatie farls and half a pint of stout!
Singing, 'Oh would ye go and are ye comin' out?
I'll buy ye fifty tatie farls and half a pint of stout!'

Crawford Howard

St Patrick and the Snakes

You've heard of the snakes in Australia,
You've heard of the snakes in Japan,
You've heard of the rattler — that old Texas battler —
Whose bite can mean death to a man.
They've even got snakes in old England —
Nasty adders all yellow and black —
But in Erin's green Isle we can say with a smile
They're away — and they're not coming back!

Now years ago things was quite different —
There was serpents all over the place.
If ye climbed up a ladder ye might meet an adder,
Or a cobra might lep at your face,
If ye went for a walk up the Shankill,
Or a dander along Sandy Row,
A flamin' great python would likely come writhin'
An' take a lump outa yer toe!

Now there once was a guy called St. Patrick,
A preacher of fame and renown —
An' he hoisted his sails and came over from Wales
To convert all the heathens in Down,
An' he hirpled about through the country
With a stick an' a big pointy hat,
An' he kept a few sheep that he sold on the cheap,
But sure there's no money in that!

He was preachin' a sermon in Comber
An gettin' quite carried away
An' he mentioned that Rome had once been his home
(But that was the wrong thing to say!)
For he felt a sharp pain in his cheek-bone
An' he stuck up a hand 'till his bake
An' the thing that had lit on his gub (an' had bit)
Was a wee Presbyterian snake!

Now the snake slithered down from the pulpit
(Expectin' St. Patrick to die),
But yer man was no dozer — he lifted his crozier
An' he belted the snake in the eye,
And he says till the snake, 'Listen legless!
You'd just better take yerself aff!
If you think that that trick will work with St. Patrick
You must be far worser nor daft!'

So the snake slithered home in a temper
An' it gathered its friends all aroun'
An' it says, 'Listen, mates! We'll get on wer skates,
I reckon it's time to leave town!
It's no fun when you bite a big fella
An' sit back and expect him to die
An' he's so flamin' quick with thon big, crooked stick
That he hits ye a dig in the eye!'

So a strange sight confronted St. Patrick
When he woke up the very next day.
The snakes with long faces were all packin' their cases
An' headin' for Donegall Quay.
Some got on cheap flights to Majorca
And some booked apartments in Spain.
They were all headin' out and there wasn't a doubt
That they weren't going to come back again.

So the reason the snakes left old Ireland,
(An' this is no word of a lie),
They all went to places to bite people's faces
And be reasonably sure that they'd die.
An' the oul' snakes still caution their grandsons,
'For God's sake beware of St. Pat!
An' take yerselves aff if you see his big staff,
An' his cloak, an' his big pointy hat!'

Crawford Howard

Billy Ritchie

Billy Ritchie, from Gilford, County Down, is a man with an exceptionally retentive memory. He is now well known throughout Northern Ireland for his delivery of long monologues by Service and Marshall and the contemporary verse of Bill Nesbitt. He is however a gifted composer in his own right and his verse often takes a wry look at society with plenty of humour and dialect thrown in!

The Thing in the Road

One windy August evening, driving with a heavy load,
On a 'straight' I spotted something in the middle of the road.
Quite merrily it bowled along, without apparent care,
As if to say, 'All nature's mine, I can go anywhere!'

Now, at this point I'd like to make, confession if I may,
To feeling mean and nasty, as I'd had a heavy day,
So I pulled the big truck t'wards it as it seemed to make a dash
And got the right front wheel in line to make a fatal squash.

I couldn't see what happened and what is furthermore
I didn't even hear a sound above the engine's roar,
But when I'd gone a little way I'd made a hit I knew,
For I could see my handiwork in the rear mirror view.

Then gleefully I gloated that I had got it right,
For it was lying all cut up, with bits of red and white!
The beast in me was happy as I went upon my way,
While in my mind I thought, 'That's one that won't go far today!'

Still now I hear your question as to just exactly what
Had got it's wanderings cut short. Was it rabbit, bird or cat,
Or maybe someone's wee pet dog, the said best friend of man.
No, none of these, I'll tell you, 'twas a Coca Cola can.

Billy Ritchie

The School Inspector

The class room was quite peaceful as all the girls and boys
Read storybooks of interest and made very little noise.
The atmosphere was happy, but it quickly turned to gloom
As entered in a man, who seemed to bring impending doom.
No introduction needed for they'd seen the face before
And most of them had sampled his crankiness and roar.
For this was an Inspector, who would hard their knowledge try.
All present shrunk and hoped that he would miss and pass them by.
His piercing eyes swept round the room and made them stiff with
    fright,
If asked a question, well they knew they'd better answer right.
Each tried to look nonchalent though inside them panic grew,
Until he glowered at Jamie Brown and said, 'I'll start with you!'
'Let's put your learning to the test and see how much you know.
'Sit up and tell me who broke down the walls of Jericho?'
Well Jamie quaked, his knees went weak, complexion turned pale
    cream.
He wondered was he having just a long nightmarish dream,
But from such possibility emerged, bereft of any joy,
As the voice of his inquisitor boomed out, 'Well tell me boy?'
So back to stern reality he jolted from his daze,
And he felt the man look through him, so ferocious was his gaze.
His mouth went dry, he shook with fear, his nerves were all at sea,
But he stammered, 'Mister, I don't know, but, sir it wasn't me!'
The Inspector was astounded and at once began to fume.
Then quickly bolted for the door and made out of the room.
He felt that seldom had he heard an answer so absurb. absurd
Outside he found the teacher and she his wrath incurred!
'Who wrecked the walls of Jericho? A question straight and prim,
I just enquired of that lad Brown — he said it wasn't him!'
The teacher felt embarrassed, but she answered with a smile,
'That wee monkey! I suppose it was him all the while!'
To get an answer quite like that made him enraged and vexed,
So up the corridor he stormed to the Headmaster next.
With righteous indignation, but his reason felt at bay,
As with disbelief he listened to what that man had to say.

For when he had recounted the details, (all correct),
The Head says, 'That lad's honest — I'd vouch that for a fact,
And though perhaps mischievous through exuberance of youth,
If he says he didn't do it — well I'd say he's told the truth!'
This overcame your man of course and in a towering rage
He wrote all in a letter and it filled a lengthy page,
With every absurb detail that his memory could afford
And he sent it off, complaining to the Education Board.
'Such ignorance!' he mumbled to himself as days went by,
Until a fortnight later he received this bland reply,
'Dear sir, though we appreciate your very real concern,
Our sole responsibility's to see that pupil's learn
And though you have our sympathy on problems with your wall,
Our department we regret can't offer help at all.
So to the Ministry of Works suggest your make your fuss,
For walls and buildings and the likes have nought to do with us!'

Billy Ritchie

The Hearing Aid

Oul' Davie McCann had been deaf many years.
What folk said he never could tell,
Then one day he spotted an advert that claimed
He could once more hear clear as a bell.

And into the bargain, with this, do ye mind,
This chip and transistor machine,
In size, shape and colour was so well designed
That in use it would never be seen.

So Dave kept the advert., (he tore it out rough),
Then made an appointment to try,
Well! Lo and behold ye! It worked right enough,
And so he decided to buy.

Now the thing seemed no more than the size of a bug,
Yet he heard all the sounds of the air,
With the gadget stuck in at the back of his lug
And covered forbye with his hair.

Thus now hearing all, Davie went on his way,
Having happily paid up the fee.
The agent says, 'Come back three months from today,
For a service and check, which are free.

'When this time was up, Dave went back, looking pleased.
Says the agent, 'It still works like new.
I'd warrant to say that your lifestyle has eased.
Your relations, I'd say, are pleased too.'

'Oh — divil the plazed,' oul' Davie replied,
'For I haven't as yet let them know.
I wanted to find out just who's on my side,
And thought 'twould be best to lie low!

'So of it these months I've said nothing at all,
But boys, I have listened me fill
Just what they think of me, I now know it all
And three times I've altered me will!'

Billy Ritchie

39

Paddy's Prayer

Paddy was a Catholic and a man of simple ways
With a Faith that seemed to carry him through life,
Emphatically believing that he who stops and prays,
Would get his needs in times of pressing strife.

When at one time Pat's affairs got something out of hand.
You may find his course of action rather odd,
But he wanted to put through a plea with no hint of demand
And so he wrote a letter straight to God.

'Dear Father, up in Heaven, you will know my need is dire,
So I trust on my request you will not frown,
But I work out at the moment that the least I do require
And appeal to You to grant us fifty poun'.

'Then he popped it in the postbox thinking, 'He will find a way.
'On the envelope he simply wrote 'To God.'
In the due course it was lifted by the middle of next day
By the postman, Billy Mac., who was a Prod.!

Now Billy bein' a member of the local Orange Lodge
Brought the matter to a meeting for to press.
'If our hearts are set in charity, let's not the issue dodge,
Can't we help Paddy in his dark distress?'

'For although he is a Catholic, he's still a decent lad,
I'm sure you all know him as well as I.
If we can't make an effort, then I'd say it's rather sad
And though funds are low, it's only right to try!

Well the matter was debated and got nearly shelved away
While charity with funding had to strive,
Until it was decided by all present there that day
That the best that they could do was 'twenty five'.

40

So the cash was sent to Paddy with a note to wish him well,
On the headed paper of the orange and blue,
Expressing their desiring of his worries for to quell
And hoping that perhaps 'twould see him through.

As Pat strolled on the roadway in a further seven days,
He met Seamus, whom he'd told about his plan.
'Just how has it been going?' with a twinkle Seamus says,
'How'd you get on with your letter till Yer Man?'

'Did you get help like you asked for in answer to your 'prayer?'
'Says Pat, 'I knew He'd help me if He could
For He always has responded to a justified affair
And He sent help to me like I knew He would.'

'Still His wisdom I now question and my faith begins to fall
And with me you'll know for certain that's no laugh,
For He sent it through the brethern of the local Orange Hall,
And would you believe? The buggers kept the half!'

Billy Ritchie

The Drunken Lad

Wee Will got a sampling of whiskey
And ended up drunk as a fool.
He was found hanging on to the railings
Encircling the Primary School.

Around him a crowd quickly gathered.
Some offered to lend him a hand,
But trying to make him walk homewards,
Was useless, he just couldn't stand.

This attracted two policemen's attention,
Who said, 'We'll take care of this lad.'
They bundled him in the patrol car
To chauffeur him back to his pad.

They were met at the door by his mother,
Who yelled, 'Disobedient wee BRAT!
You were told to be home here by tea-time,
So to learn you, just take that and that!'

Then she hammered him round by the table,
With a left after right round the lugs,
Till a swipe that went wild hit the dresser
And brought down a plate and two mugs.

'Now look what has happened!' she guldered,
'Of that broken delf you're the cause.
If you give me an ounce more of bother
I'll take it and wallop your jaws!'

'So sit down on that chair in the corner,
And be quiet, with no if or but,
For you're shaping to be like your father,
And he was a drunken wee scut!'

'And another thing — wasting your money,
You'd squander it all so you would.
If your hangover's bad in the morning
May the devil of it give you good!'

At that she left off the barging
And back to the policemen she strolled.
'I think that will sort out the matter,
At times lads must be well controlled!'

The policemen just gaped in amazement,
But later they giggled with glee,
For the 'lad' was a wee man of sixty,
And his mother a spritely ninety-three!

Billy Ritchie

Firework Frolics

You can't buy fireworks in Belfast,
They've been banned this few years past,
But none the less you'll hear the din
Of those that have been smuggled in
From places over in the South,
Particularly County Louth.
This tale's of such a smuggler's load.
A lady from the Oldpark Road
Who went, according to the talk
On an excursion to Dundalk.
It being near to Hallowe'en
Decided to procure a wheen
Of squibs and bangers from a store,
And powerful rockets by the score.
Such bit of shopping being done,
Her problems really now begun,
To bring her haul North in one piece
Past customs, army and the police.
The best way seemed to her in haste
Was tie the whole lot round her waist.
Thus she fixed them right around
With all the rockets pointing down,
Made sure that none would slip or flop
By wearing corsets on the top.
With coat pulled tightly round her back,
She looked just like spuds in a sack.
A fancy cape kept out the rain,
Thus clad, she headed for the train.
The journey was without event.
Back in her street she felt content,
Reaching home could now relax,
Having bluffed two army checks.
Stood bragging in her living room,
How they'd be seeing fireworks soon,
Little dreaming as she gloated,
T'would be sooner than she thought it,

For as she boasted of her ruse
A fire spark lit a rocket fuse,
Which firing threw her on the floor
And zoomed her through the open door.
Thus several others also lit,
Speeding her up quite a bit.
The thrust this gave was quite enough
To, with her cape spread, take right off
With such a great increase in power
To reach a thousand miles an hour.
She realised her path of flight
When going past a satellite,
Creating every way she went
Confusion in the firmament.
Astronomers were on their toes
With wide reports of U.F.O's,
While worried N.A.S.A. experts met
Computer data prints to vet,
To try and figure out just why
This object swished around the sky.
The Russians looked on in dismay,
With urgent calls to U.S.A.
As jumping jacks began to burn
She took a sudden downward turn,
Coming back t'wards earth again,
Amidst a shower of golden rain,
As homewards o'er the coast she sped
A passing seagull shook its head.
By using cape she tried to steer
With lowered feet, like landing gear,
But catching power lines by her boots
Pulled up two pylons by the roots
Cables touched as through she tore
Causing flashing arcs galore.
While this display lit up the night
People talked of Northern Lights.
Doomsday preachers gazed on high
Declaring that the end was nigh.

Then swooping low, she cut it fine
And cleared the washing off a line,
But over home she felt a pain
And yelled, 'I'll circle round again.
A hose I urgently require,
I'm sure my bloomers are on fire!
Better hurry! Understand?
Before the blaze gets out of hand.
If that should happen I'm afraid
You'll have to call the Fire Brigade.'
They hosed her out the next time round,
And in attempting to touch down
In front of crowds turned out to watch
She landed in a cabbage patch,
But coming just too quickly in
She gouged the lawn up with her chin.
As final rockets fizzled out
The crowds let out a mighty shout.
Dishevelled she lay in repose
Entangled in that line of clothes.
The kids all gave a mighty cheer.
'We hope you'll do the same next year!'

Billy Ritchie

The Ghostly Footsteps

I tripped and fell the other day.
A couple of companions laughed,
Though I had only strained me foot
Ye know, the pain near driv me daft.

But later that subsided
And I was feeling rightly
I shaped to on me ceili go
As I do almost nightly.

But here, although the pain had eased
It left a mighty swollen foot.
Says I, 'I can't go out like this
Because I can't put on me boot.'

Then inspiration came to me
To go and have a look around
'till hidden in the attic space
Surprise — me Grandad's boots I found.

Now Grandad was a great big man,
By most accounts near six foot seven.
His size of boots appeared to me
To be e'en bigger than eleven.

I pulled one on my swollen foot
And feeling I looked rather odd,
With one foot big, the other small,
I started walking down the road.

The night was still, the road seemed dark
Though lighted by a crescent moon,
By lighted paths, through wreaths of mist,
I made my way into the gloom.

But prior to my getting far
My ears detected something wrong.
It seemed I heard another step
Like someone walked with me along.

Though when I stopped and listened
I couldn't hear a sound
While with my now adjusted eyes
Could see that no-one was around.

Continuing to hobble on
I knew I heard that step again.
As fear welled up I quite forgot
Any residue of pain.

Stopping in the silence,
I stood listening in the hush,
Expecting ghostly figures
To emerge from every bush.

The hairs upon me neck stood up,
I broke out in a prickly sweat.
Shivers ran along me spine,
I shudder to think of it yet.

But then I solved the mystery.
You may doubt it, but it's true,
For every step the big boot took,
The wee one, keeping up took two!

Billy Ritchie

The Dental 'Monster'

He looked in with his mirror just to see what he could find.
'Uh Huh!', he said, like one who ought to know,
But when the drill he lifted and began with it to grind,
I could picture molars rotting by the row.

He scraped and scratched for ages, then he blasted in some air,
Then the fillings in, I asked if I could go
Out, although he'd done the cavities and finished them with care,
My enquiry brought the awful answer, 'No!'

'There's a tooth beyond redemption, that may be to your surprise.'
Was the way he said it, in his line of tact.
Then produced a wicked needle right before my anxious eyes
And informed me that he must the tooth extract.

Well, as he advanced towards me, with the needle at a poise
The toothache seemed to be of less degree.
I swear that from his throat there came a sort of laughing noise
And in his eye I caught a glint of glee.

A quick jag, then another, then my face felt awful queer
And, you may doubt my theory, but it's true.
It seemed like he was trying to instil me full of fear
For next I saw the forceps loom in view.

Like some outrageous monster he advanced upon me there,
I, scared as though I knew I'd had my call,
But as he closed towards me, sure I nearly jumped the chair
And I knocked the pliers slam against the wall.

But the job must be completed and he had to see it through.
He recovered and he came my way again
Now seeming twice the monster, with a threat of what he'd do
While desire for flight was balanced by the pain.

When he reached in with thon levers and began to make the draw
The root seemed like a metre of the best,
For although the pain was dampened, still the gum felt somewhat raw
As he tugged and pushed, his knee against me chest!

But then the pull was finished and at last the tooth was out,
With the hole packed up with bits of cotton wool,
Then I got around to wonder what I'd been afraid about,
And to tell the truth, I felt a bloomin' fool!

Today I met that dentist while out walking on the road,
Where he didn't give me call to speed my pace,
For his wave was very friendly and his cheery smile was broad,
Nothing like some monster out of space!

Now, with toothache gone, recovery is well upon its way
When I think, upon reflection, I now find
That the most appalling creature that I saw the other day
Was really just a monster in me mind.

Still, when I remember reading of a certain Mister Hyde,
Who in his monstrous evil ran amok,
I'm convinced that Doctor Jeckyll only showed another side
And was really more a dentist than a Doc!

Billy Ritchie

The Henpecked Workaholic

In matters concerning employment
Some people take me to the fair,
For some are heart feart of their bosses
While others are 'devil may care'.

In the former group fell Eck Delaney.
He was scared stiff of getting the sack.
The reason was clear, he was henpecked,
By a wife who was ne'er off his back.

Oh! A nark who was all overbearing,
While he lacked the fight of a mouse.
He'd have worked round the clock day and nightly
If just to keep out of the house!

Well as it so happened one winter,
While working the late six till two,
One night about five to eleven,
He complained he was taking the 'flu.

Says Jimmy, his mate, 'Go home early,
With a night's early rest you'll be fine.
No need for a loss in your wages,
I'll clock out your card when it's time.'

Says Eck, 'The idea seems tempting,
But still in my mind there's a doubt,
I'm afraid if the boss was to see me,
Or maybe in some way find out.'

'Ach! Divil the find out,' says Jimmy,
'Of that now you need have no fright,
For he's away home till his supper,
And he surely won't be back tonight!'

51

Well, he left with a kind of reluctance,
His nerves being somewhat on edge,
With his collar turned up, he walked — furtive
And sticking in close to the hedge.

When he got home the house was in darkness.
Thinks he, 'Now the wife's fast asleep,
I'll go in real quiet, not to wake her,
And up to the bedroom I'll creep.'

He tiptoed upstairs very quietly,
But then got the shock of his life,
For what does he see through the doorway,
But the boss was in bed with his wife!

You'll find it strange how he reacted
For he tiptoed back down, holding breath,
Ran all the way back to the workshop,
Puffed and looking the colour of death.

Says Jimmy, 'Whatever's the matter?
You're looking both pale and distraught.'
Says Eck, 'Man, you talk of a near thing!
Do you know, I was nearly bein' caught!'

Billy Ritchie

52

Maud Steele

Maud Steele is a primary school teacher from Kilrea, County Derry but for the past few years she has become much sought after as a speaker at social gatherings from Womens' Institute meetings to church soirees where audiences have doubled up upon hearing her hilarious verses. Maud's use of the 'vernacular' and acute observations of the human condition ensures that her listeners are giggling even before she dawns her overall and headscarf.

The Disillusioned Dreamer

Ye know sometimes, I'm just about scunnered,
Wi' workin' and slavin' all day,
Lookin' after a man and a family,
That gives ye no thanks, and no pay.

When I think of the dreams of me young days,
Floatin' down a long aisle, dressed in white,
Being adored by a handsome young husband,
Who'd rush home to me arms every night.

Boys ye must be clean daft, when ye're youthful,
Tae imagine these dreams will come true,
Ye don't think o' the dishes and nappies,
And nobody tae wash them, but you!

You pitied the successful career girl,
You just thought, 'Och, she can't get a man!'
You even felt that bit superior,
Because you had proved that you CAN!

'But now when she's winin' and dinin',
Or enjoyin' the sunshine in Spain,
And your oul' boy's tuk off wi' his cronies,
You're left in the house, wi' the wean.

When you're chained tae the sink, and it's rainin',
And the weans are all fightin' as well,
Oh, what would you give for her life now?
Or even just half an hour, tae yersel'.

Ye spend yer days cookin' and cleanin'
Ye can't even go to the loo,
Without somebody yellin' for mammy,
Ye would think ye had gone to Peru!

The T.V. is your sole entertainment,
An' when ye get time to look at the screen,
You're over to sleep in five minutes,
And wakenin' up when they're playin' 'The Queen.'

Ye compare your oul' boy wi' the heroes,
An' you'll admit that he's no Movie Star,
But when all's said and done, if you're honest,
Aren't ye better wi' him than J.R.?

When ye view the object of yer passion,
Lyin' snorin' in front of the telly,
Och yer heart would still give a wee flutter,
In spite of his chins and beer belly.

And that face that looks back in the mirror,
Is not all that IT used to be
But he never says one word about it,
At least, well, he disn't tae me.

I suppose I should not be complainin'
But a moan does ye good, by a time,
We're a sight better off than some others,
I thank God we're not on the breadline.

And if I was twenty the morrow,
And had me life over again,
I suppose, I would do, what I'm doin',
I wouldn't be without him or the weans!

Maud Steele

Surprise, Surprise

Ye cud 'a knocked me down wi' a feather,
When me oul' boy walked in through the door,
Wi' a Valentine card an' red roses,
Sure I nearly fell down through the floor.

Eighteen Valentines Days I'd kep' hopin,
For some flowers or a card, but no fear,
'Ye don't bother wi' that when ye're married.'
Was his lame oul' excuse every year.

But what's prompted this romantic gesture?
What's he lookin' or what's on his mind?
(Isn't it desperate to be that suspicious)
But the answer I'm anxious to find.

Och maybe all them T.V. adverts,
Have at last filtered throught till his brain,
An' persuaded him flowers for the missus,
From yappin' might make her refrain!

But, middle age makes men go — funny!
So, I better just mind what I say,
An' be thankful it's me that's got roses,
Or there'll be none next Valentine's Day!

Maud Steele

Aw, Have a Heart!

Looking after ourselves, was what we had in mind,
When we went to the class, and our names we all signed.
We sat on the floor, got to know one another,
And discussed what we hoped this new class had to offer.

We looked for our pulses and felt round and round.
Some felt they had snuffed it, when no pulse they found,
But Mary assured them they'd nothin to fear,
And a digital monitor clipped on their ear.

We talked about eating a healthier diet,
And with Wednesday night zeal, we decided to try it.
We must cut our intake of salt, sugar and fat,
And the faithful oul' chip pan? Well, goodbye to that!

The folly of drinkin and smokin we've learned,
And to sensible habits, we no doubt have turned.
We're now reading food labels, instead of good books,
We're starving our minds, to improve on our looks.

We've cut out the drink and the fags — signed the pledge.
We're livin' on 'All Bran', skim milk, fruit and veg,
And while doubtless the value of fibre we're proving,
Some have found the experience, a little TOO moving!

We've clenched up our buttocks, and held tummies in,
And learned to touch walls with our nose or our chin,
We've strengthened our arms, our abdomens and thighs,
With half squats and press ups, loud creakings and sighs!

With a tape and a chart, we have checked body fat,
And discovered we're obese! Well just fancy that!
But when energy levels seemed likely to dip,
Mary passed round the oranges,, to perk us all up.

Then she set pulses racing, with an exercise bike,
Which took us to nowhere and back in one night!
The bench steppin' proved kinda hard on the legs,
But it sure made us glad we weren't still on the fegs!

We've tried joggin' and skippin, we've tried hoppin, too,
But this leaping about made us dash to the loo!
We hope all this effort will make our hearts stronger,
And if we keep it up, perhaps we will live longer.

Then we lay on our backs, and we tried to relax,
And it's hard when your mind keeps on turnin' to snacks,
But when lights were switched off, Mary's voice was so soothing
It took all our will power to keep us from snoozing!

Back home we undid all the good we had done
With a Mars bar or two, or a big fresh cream bun,
But decided, tomorrow we'd stop all this cheating,
And make a serious effort at healthier eating.

We've booklets and leaflets, and charts for the wall,
It'll take us to Christmas to read through them all!
And if dedication, some of us did lack,
Sure we came along anyway, just for the crack!

Maud Steele

Washday Wonder

Well I'm hanged if I know where they go to,
But disappear they surely do,
Every time that I'm doin' the washin'
I hae one, an' there ought to be two!

Do you think they dissolve in the water?
I just cannot know where they have gone,
When I hoak them out after I've washed them,
Instead of each pair, I hae one!

An' it isn't just once in a wonder,
But the same oul' thing week after week,
D'ye know it's just drivin' me crazy,
Them socks, playing hide an' go seek.

Every time that I look in the basket,
There seems to be more and still more,
An' not even two of them matches,
Wud it not nearly make yer head sore!

By now I have quite a collection
Of socks every colour an' creed
D'ye think when ye put them together,
Is it possible, single socks BREED?

Maud Steele

Damsel in Distress

I was out on me own in the motor,
An' this rumlin' noise comes to me ears,
An' the steerin' starts twistin, and draggin',
A flat tyre! That confirmed me worst fears.

So I pulled in an' jumped out to check it,
An' a right fool I started to feel,
For I hadn't a clue where the jack went,
An' I HOPED I had got a spare wheel!

Then I noticed I'd parked in a puddle,
An' of course it had started to rain,
I wud a needed a divin' suit wi' me,
If that wheel I was goin' tae change!

I thought I would stan' an' luk helpless,
An some kind soul wud come to me aid,
But the cars all whizzed past about 60,
Sendin' splashes right over me head.

People say that ye shouldn't be drivin'
If ye can't change a wheel by yersel'
I'll admit that they've got a good point there,
But up to now I had managed quite well.

I started to prise off the hub cap,
An' got meself covered in glar,
I tried a wee twist at the wheel nuts,
But I couldn't shift them very far!

Them oul' power tools they use at the garage,
Put the nuts on tight as can be,
An' as I've not got muscles like Tarzan,
They'd no hope o' bein' shifted by me!

Then I thought, 'I have friends in the district,
They just live down the road a wee bit.'
So I locked up and started off joggin'.
Was I glad I had gone to Keep Fit!

I arrived and explained my position,
An' they soon had me problem in hand,
Thank God, there's still folk in the country,
Tae help ye, when ye're in a jam!

But the thought of it still makes me shudder,
When I think where I might hae been stuck,
In the middle of moss, up a mountain,
I would surely have been out of luck!

So I'll just have to take a few lessons,
They say bein' prepared always pays,
An gallant knights, lookin' damsels to rescue,
Are kinda thin on the groun' nowadays!

Maud Steele

Do It Yersel'

Wud you credit that some folk could be so handless,
Seems the only one CAN do some jobs is YOU,
I mean simple things that wouldn't take an expert,
Like fittin' on a new roll in the loo!

But naw, ye'll find it sittin, on the cistern,
Or rollin' round the floor among yer feet,
When it really wouldn't take a powerful effort,
To fit it, without gettin' off yer seat!

I scoul, complain an' girn until I'm scunnered,
But I might as well keep quate, not waste me time,
For when that roll gets right down tae the cardboard,
Ye can guess whose hands'll change it, they'll be MINE

Maud Steele

Meg's Memory

(or Multistorey Mix-up)

Now Meg had a terrible memory,
She just could not mind where things wus,
She spent her life lookin' and searchin'
For handbags, or car keys or gloves.

Mind, she put things away in a 'safe place',
But then it would just leave her mind,
And when she was goin' out shoppin',
Her handbag she just could not find.

She'd try hard to think where she'd put it,
She'd search high and low, up and down,
But, as often as not when she'd found it,
Not one shop was still open in town.

She would go up the street for a lettuce,
And come back wi' tomatoes instead,
Sometimes she'd come home wi' potatoes,
When what she went out for was bread.

It was just the same thing wi' the letters,
Ye know, like bills we all get,
She'd stuff them away in a cupboard,
And then, yes of course, she'd forget!

They would come to switch off her electric,
Because she'd forgotten to pay,
She just could not know where that bill went,
Though she minded it came in one day!

Now Meg she just loved a day's shoppin',
In Belfast or Coleraine, ye know,
So one day she got in the motor,
The Tower Centre was where she would go.

But when she got up to the 'Centre',
Thon big tower block park loomed ahead,
There wasn't a space on the ground floor,
So on up the levels she sped.

At last she was lucky, she parked it,
Remembered to lock it all round,
The bargains were waitin' to tempt her,
So she got in the lift and flew down.

She came back two hours later, exhausted,
Her shoppin' bag trailin' the ground,
She pressed at the button for ages,
But the oul' lift just wouldn't come down.

In a while she was that scunnered waitin',
She thought she'd go up stairs instead.
There seemed to be hundreds and hundreds,
And her oul' feet were feelin' like lead.

At last through a door oul' Meg staggered,
The one that was marked Level 3,
To where she was quite sure she'd parked it,
But no car of hers did she see.

Then Meg, she flew into a panic,
'Me poor wee Fiesta!' she wailed,
'Some bad boy's run aff wi' me motor,
The VILLAN, he ought to be jailed!

"Send for the polis!' she shouted,
'Me poor wee Fiesta's been stole,
There's some bad boys about Ballymena,
Oh! What brought me up to this hole?'

The police took her back to the station,
To get a few details put down,
'Don't worry too much, there, there madam,
We have our suspicions. Sit down.'

The policeman said, 'What is your number?'
'It's E I naw, that was the last,
Och Mister, I'm hopeless wi' numbers,
Ye'll just have to phone Jimmy and ask!.'

'Well, what is your phone number Madam?'
'Kilrea four, o, Lord I can't mind.'
So they had to get out a big phone book,
And check it out line after line.

Well, at last they got down all the details,
The number, the colour, the make,
The time she came in and her address,
By now it was getting quite late.

Just then a big policeman came over,
He said, 'Madam, we've just found your car.'
'Oh thank God,' said Meg, 'Ye's are good uns,'
I hope thon boy didn't get far!'

'I suspect that it's just where YOU left it,
On level FIVE as you will see,
You were one floor too low, sorry madam,
You were looking for your car on THREE!'

'Your memory is not too good madam
So next time you need some new shoes,
Just stick to Kilrea for your shopping,
Stay there, 'til your memory improves!

So girls, if you'll all take a warnin',
If to thon Tower Centre, ye'es head,
Take note of the level ye're parked on,
And don't end up in bother like Meg.

Maud Steele

Rest in Peace
(Some chance!)

I woke up wi' a cough an' a splutter,
And this terrible ache in me head,
I staggered across to the bathroom,
Then decided I'd go back to bed.

'I don't think I'll get up this mornin' '
I groaned, 'I have got a right dose.'
'Just lie there,' says James, 'I'll go down now,
And make a wee cup o' tay an' some toast.'

'O.K.', I said, 'Just get the weans up.'
An' lay back in bed wi' a sigh,
The next thing I heard a voice shoutin'
'Hi Mammy, did you see my tie?'

I said, 'Naw, did ye look in yer bedroom?'
He says, 'Aye, but I don't see it there,'
So I trailed out o' bed and looked for it,
An' pulled it out from the back of a chair.

I had just settled down when the phone rang,
And nobody seemed to hear it but me,
An' no wonder, for sure ye'd hear nothin'
For the noise blarin' from the T.V.

But still that oul' phone kept on ringin',
'till I just couldn't stand any more,
So I struggled up, goin' to answer it,
And it stopped as me feet touched the floor.

I'd just snuggled back under the blankets,
When another head popped round the door,
She said, 'Mammy, I need dinner money.'
So I put me feet back on the floor.

An' I hoaked in me purse for the money,
Then lay back to rest me poor head,
When the weest boy climbed out of his cot,
Sayin', 'Mammy, I'll sleep in your bed!'

So he jumped in and tramped on me stomach,
Then poked at me eyes, pulled me hair,
Then he started to kick off the bedclothes,
'till he nearly drove me to despair.

Then below, I heard not such sweet music,
The recorder! Boys that thing's a curse!
If ye have a sore head, a recorder,
Being played, makes it feel ten times worse!

So at last I just gave up the struggle,
And went down in me oul' dressing gown,
Says James, 'Are ye feelin' a bit better?
Sure I didn't expect you to come down!'

'Feelin' better?' I snapped, 'Glad ye think so!'
An' I near ate the face of me spouse,
'Y'ed get more peace to sleep at the Diamond,
Than ye'd get to rest here in this house!'

Maud Steele

Granny's Pilgrimage to Church Island

We were sittin' half dozin' one Sunday,
Says James, 'Maud this isn't much fun,
We'll go to Rasharkin for Granny,
And see if she'll go for a run.'

The day it was dull, a bit drizzley,
The patches of blue sky were few,
We set off to Rasharkin for Granny,
And big Alfie came along too.

We headed on up to New Ferry
To watch all the boys water ski,
We went out round for a wee dander,
Intendin' to go home for tea.

But what should we spy, but Church Island,
Says James, 'Have ye'se ever been there?
Gran and Alfie said, 'No we have never,
We could go there now, if it would fair.'

So we got in the car and we drove round,
A wee bendy road, not too far,
We looked for the way to get down there,
Found a slap, and in there parked the car.

We walked down the road to a stone wall,
'Ye have to climb over.' says Jim,
Grannie says, 'Och Jamesie, ye'er jokin',
Are ye sure that's the only way in?'

So after a bit of a struggle,
We got ourselves over the wall,
James and Alfie set off at a canter,
And we couldn't keep up, not at all.

But we just went along at our leisure,
After all, we were out for the day,
When we heard a wild roarin' behind us,
Saw a herd of cows headin' our way.

We looked all around for escape routes,
But divil the one could we find,
To the right was a sheugh and barbed wire,
The only way out was behind!

Now Granny, she started to panic,
For out on the left was a marsh,
I don't like the look o' that white cow,
I think it's her's roarin' the worst!

'Oh, my God it's a bull!' shouted Granny,
And she took to her heels at a run,
But the cattle kept followin' after,
'till Granny, Lord help her, was done.

Just then we had come to some marshland,
We started to sink in quite deep,
'Oh! We're going to be drowned!' yelled poor granny,
As the shoes were sucked clean off her feet.

She said 'It's a judgement upon us,
For we're breakin' the Lord's Sabbath Day,
Trespassin' on someboby's property,
It's the price of us, that's what I say!'

But still that did not solve the problem,
The bull was still catching up fast,
When what do you think, but a big cow,
Just happened to go amblin, past.

It diverted the big bull's attention,
Says Granny, 'Now this is our chance!'
So we turned round and faced all his followers
And d'ye know what? They all ran off at once!

'Me poor heart is all of a flutter'
Says Granny, 'When I leave this field,
Ye'll not get ME back to Church Island,
For I thought sure me fate had been sealed!'

So back up the field we all trotted,
And spraghled back over the wall,
We vowed never again to break Sunday,
Or go in a field with a BULL!

Maud Steele

Forty! Who's Countin'

Well, I'm goin' tae be forty the morrow,
And sure forty is not all that oul,
But ye hear some brat callin' ye an oul' doll,
And ye feel ye could knock him out coul'.

But when ye have time tae think o'er it,
Ye can mind what you thought of it still,
That most folk were past it at thirty,
And at forty they were over the hill!

Now it always had been my ambition,
Tae reach forty without a grey hair,
So if one came to my attention,
I'd make sure it did not stay long there.

But I'll relax after the morrow,
And let meself grow old with grace,
For ye always know ones that's been tintin'
It just doesn't match their oul' face!

And Lord! Not another wee wrinkle!
I never saw that one before,
So I'll buy some of that 'Oil of Ulay',
And hope it prevents any more.

Some people say, 'Don't call them wrinkles,
It's nicer to say "Laughter Lines"!'
If that was what done it, I'm tellin' ye,
I must a had some quare laughs in me time!

Ye might catch a glimpse of your reflection,
In them shop mirrors as ye go through,
And for a second it just doesn't hit ye,
That thon middle-aged woman, is YOU!

Ye run into some childhood acquaintance,
She may be dressed up in jewels and fur,
But ye spot the grey hairs and you're thinkin'
'Boys! I'm stickin' it better than her!'

While you're sayin' 'Hello, and how are ye?'
And she's saying somethin' the same,
Ye're racking yer brains, but it's useless,
For ye just can't remember her name!

And as ye retreat in confusion,
Ye start thinkin' 'Me memory's gone!
Is this the onset of me dotage?'
Now there's something to ponder upon!

The weans think I'm just an oul' fogey,
They now won't wear one thing that I choose,
Their eyes open wide in pure horror,
Sayin' 'I wouldn't be seen DEAD in them
    shoes!'

But some people hold other opinions,
They say your life's only begun,
When ye reach that 4, 0, you should venture,
To find your own place in the sun.

But, the back's a bit dodgy, the eyes a bit dim,
And of youth I have not found the fountain,
So tomorrow they'll say, 'Are ye forty today?'
I'll say, 'Aye, I'm just forty. Who's countin' '

Maud Steele

Knock, Knock! Who's There?

I was just home from work, an' the house was a mess,
When who comes to the back door? Oh you'll never guess,
The Reverend Thingmajig, new to the town
An' wan of the elders thought they would — call round!

I don't know what I said as they came through the door,
For me eyes kep' on strayin' tae the mess round the floor,
I felt that embarrased, as I looked at me feet,
For I'm tellin' you my kitchen was far from bein' neat!

The sink, full of dishes, an' clothes on the chairs,
Books an toys by the dozen, an' shoes! three or four pair!
They said, 'We were passing and thought we'd drop in,'
But what I was thinkin' was surely a sin!
(I haven't a thing in the house, if they stay,
Oh! what will I do if I have to make tay?)

They said, 'We're in a hurry.' an' of that I was glad,
For a seat to sit down on just couldn't be had,
They hoped they would see me at church the next week,
An' I felt that affronted, I hardly could speak!

If ye had the house shinin', an' as neat as a pin,
Ye could bet yer last penny, not wan soul would come in.
So if you're feelin' lonely, an' company ye'd like,
Then take my advice, just bring in an oul' bike,
Three or four newspapers, toys by the score,
An' scatter them liberally, all roun' the floor,
Forget about hooverin', leave the dishes undone,
An' I'll guarantee ye, dozens of people will come!

Maud Steele

The Diet Drops Out

This slimmin', I thought I had cracked it,
I had lost half a stone, maybe more,
Then we had them oul' bloomin' wet summers,
An' the pounds piled back on by the score.

For sure, what can ye do when it's rainin',
An' on holiday you're meant to be,
Instead of spenin' yer time outside walkin',
Ye'd go into a cafe for tea!

An as you queued up at the counter,
The temptation proved too much for you,
Ye'd grab a cream bun, as you're passin',
Or a slice of Black Forest Gateau!

Then this feelin' of guilt came upon ye,
Ye thought, 'Wan time can't do me much harm,'
Then picked up a few chocolate biscuits,
Tho' your calorie counter'd sounded the alarm.

But as wan bad day followed another,
An' they kept gettin' wetter, an' wetter,
Ye thought, fish an' chips, or hamburgers,
Would perhaps make ye feel a bit better.

The weans were all girnin' an yappin',
For sweeties or ice cream, or Coke,
An' ye sat in the car, an ye ate them,
Though the thought of it now, makes ye boke!

Ye remembered all your good intentions,
Tae get yer body back under control,
But the puddles were fillin' the roadway,
So it put ye off goin' for a stroll.

Now the hand on the scales shows an increase,
An' you're gettin' to the end of your tether,
So if somebody says, 'Boys, you're putting on weight!'
Just blame it all on the bad weather!

Maud Steele

The Santa Claus Syndrone

it can be

D'ye see Christmas? ~~It's only~~ a nuisance,
I'm browned aff long before it gets here,
Wi' shoppin' and panickin' and rushin',
An' everything now's got that dear!

The weans have been crakin' for months now,
This whole Santa thing is a cod,
Ye cud run yersel' intae fortune,
Tae convince them it's not a big fraud.

They see all this overpriced rubbish,
Advertised everyday on T.V.
An' it's, 'Mammy, will Santa bring me that?'
Ye wud think that ye got it all free!

There's all this keepin' up wi' the Jones's,
'Wee Jimmy's gettin' a BMX bike,
An wee Laura's gettin' a Cabbage Patch Kid doll,
An' a big pram.' Did y'iver hear the like?

An' John there, he wants a computer,
That costs two hundred poun' maybe more,
An May wants a T.V. for her own room,
Boys, wouldn't weans make yer head sore?

But, I wonder if these fancy presents,
Will bring half the excitement we got,
As we crept down on Christmas mornin'
And discovered our big lumpy sock?

Boys, we danced wi' delight, when we foun' out
That oul' Santa had come after all,
And brought us a sock full of presents,
The more now, they would seem very small.

We would hoke out a pencil and rubber,
A paintbox, a hankie, a book,
A wee bag of gold chocolate money,
An' an apple and orange from the foot.

We were happy wi' these simple items,
The weans now wud say, 'That's not fair!'
But Santa Claus brought us great pleasure,
An' he didn't have tae be a millionaire!

But the weans will grow up in a few years,
An' wi' Santa they'll no longer fuss,
An' Hi! Christmas lost most of its magic,
Since Santa stopped comin' tae us!

So perhaps it IS worth all the bother,
Tae make some of their wee dreams come true,
And give THEM somethin' nice tae look back on
When they're ouler, like me, an like you.

Maud Steele

Cold Turkey

What the heck do ye do wi' a turkey,
When all the best bits hae been ate?
An' the longer you look at the carcass,
The more an' more scunnered ye get.

But it seems such a pity to waste it,
An' throw it straight out in the bin,
So ye try to compose a new recipe,
Where ye can slip all them oul' brown bits in.

So ye chop up some mushrooms an' onions,
An ye stir up a nice curry mix,
Then ye lob in the turkey left-overs,
And hey presto! a dinner for six!

It's not bad served wi' rice white an' fluffy,
Ye're a cookery genius, that's plain!
The weans take one look at the dinner,
An' say, 'Heavens, not turkey again!'

Maud Steele

The Fitness Fanatic

If ye want tae survive and be healthy,
Ye must get up and do exercise,
Well, that was the thought that came to me,
When thon big Keep Fit Poster I spied.

It said 7. 30 on Wednesdays,
Come on now and join in the fun,
I vowed to be fitter for Christmas,
So I went to the class and signed on!

A collection of ladies had gathered,
Clad in sportswear of all sorts and kinds,
Some had figures as skinny as beanpoles,
Some had, well, more mature ones, like mine!

A slim young thing appeared on the platform,
Wi' a tape player clutched in her hand,
She outlined all the moves she expected
Us tae do when the music began.

We kicked off wi' a bit o' head rollin',
And joggin' tae loosen our knees,
This isn't too bad, I was thinkin',
For I hadn't even started tae wheeze!

But, 'That's just a warm up,' she told us,
'There's something more strenuous to come,
Just do twenty or so Jumping Jacks now,
And then walk round the floor, on yer bum!'

From that we went on to the stretchin',
And touchin' our hands tae the groun',
And bendin' and rockin' and rollin',
And burlin' our arms roun' and roun'.

Me poor oul legs now were protestin',
But she hadn't finished, Oh no!
It was, 'Down on the floor, stretch your legs up,
And now let them down, very slow.'

We had a short break tae recover,
And I wiped off the sweat from me brow,
Me poor battered body was achin',
I was beginnin' tae regret me rash vow.

The first part was bad, but by hokey!
It was nothin' compared tae the next,
She near killed us wi' skippin' an dancin',
And when nine o'clock came we weren't vexed!

Me face was as red as a beetroot,
And me legs were as limp as a rag,
And back home I managed tae stagger,
And fell back in the bath, like a bag.

By Friday, the oul' joints had stiffened,
I've spent all weekend feelin' a wreck,
But, on Wednesday, I'll dig out me track suit,
And to that Keep Fit, I'll go back!

For ye know, I will not let it beat me,
I'll jog, and I'll skip and I'll run,
And by Christmas NO ONE will be fitter,
When is that Belfast Marathon?

Maud Steele